ONE FROM 67

COLM QUINN

PUBLISHED BY
LAPWING PUBLICATIONS
c/o DENNIS & RENE GREIG
1 BALLYSILLAN DRIVE
BELFAST BT14 8HQ

PRINTED BY

TEXTFLOW SERVICES
SCIENCE LIBRARY
LENNOXVALE
MALONE ROAD, BELFAST
TEL: 663591

ISBN 1 898472 24 6
LAPWING POETRY PAMPHLET
COLM QUINN: ONE FROM 97
PUBLISHED 1995
COPYRIGHT REMAINS WITH AUTHOR

Lapwing Publications gratefully acknowledge the financial assistance of the Arts Council of Northern Ireland and The UK Foundation for Sport and the Arts in the publication of this pamphlet.

CONTENTS

IF YOU STAY IN THE HOUSE LONG ENOUGH	7
LIFERS	9
WHEATEN WARS	10
SHORT SCENE ONE	11
DOCTER'S DAUGHTER - LABOURER'S SON	12
SHORT SCENE TWO	16
UNCLE, NEPHEW, MOTHER AND SON	17
A CHICKEN FOR A CHRISTMAS DINNER	25
A WORD OR TWO ON THE SUCCESS OF MR. JEAN CLAUDE VAN DAMME	26
BEFORE BED	27
BANG AND CLATTER # 1	28
BANG AND CLATTER # 2	29
FOREVER MODERNE MARGARET	30
THEIR ARDGLASS	33
THE KING BENEATH THE CLOCK	37
OUR GRANDMOTHER'S 95TH	38
THE WAR CRIMES OF WINNIE	40
MASS PALS	40
A NOTION OF FUTURE WITHOUT HER	41
THE SHIRT I GAVE HER	42
THREE MONTHS FREE	43
WHAT KEEPS HER	44
CAUGHT SHORT	44

for
Brian, Lizzie, Virginia.

IF YOU STAY IN THE HOUSE LONG ENOUGH

If you stay in the house
All a long night,
Living with someone
And breathing their fumes,
You find yourself battling
From time to time
With the person or people in it.
I have a special enemy,
An old woman
Some decades older
Than me.
The war we waged has
Currently ran its ground
Into a siege of age and deafness,
With a no win situation.

Between the both of us,
Life is never easy.
Recently she began a dirty tricks campaign:
Not flushing the toilet
And using my toothbrush
To scrub her perspex molars.
So I moved the brush
To the top of a nearby wardrobe
And decided to let
Height win this battle.

My enemy out foxed me
The other morning when she claimed
the tooth brush fell on her head
As she walked by.
She had used it again.
'You're using it!.....Admit it!'
'You're a liar!' She roared.
'Don't use it again!'
'GET OUT!!'

There are times
When I pray for her death;
And then when we are at peace.....
I hope she never goes.
'Just get out!'
This is an honest request on her part.
You know.....
One
Day
I'm
Gonna
Do
Just
That.

LIFERS

She contradicts the popular image of old age being like
a candle stub awaiting a winter wind to end her days.
That woman is a raging stone furnace that has burned a
 hole
from the year 1898 ..... She thinks age is a licence for heavy
 words.

*'I despise the very ground you walk upon .... and
 furthermore*
I'll tell you what I'll do. If you won't get out of my house ...
then I'll go ... Yes I'll leave you to rot here, because I can't
stomach the sight of your ugly face much longer ...'

This tirade occurs when you need it least, can stomach it
 least.
I look to her eyes, and it's hard to believe we are related.
'Granny, where's this coming from ... ?'
'Look, one of us will have to go ... AND THAT'S ALL THERE
 IS TO IT'

She turns to discuss my eviction with herself, ensuring
 beforehand
That her hearing aid is switched off to all insults.
No matter how loud you scream, she cannot hear, but
 continues talking
And whistling the first notes of a flat tune that enters her
 head.

This tactic is designed to aggravate ... and it does.
Tomorrow I get to whistle through her migraine
And pretend to be deaf ..... The casualties continue.

WHEATEN WARS

Believing in one last favour before the grave, I obliged her request
and collected the four wheaten loaves from the little homestead
bakery, one half mile from the direction of my journey;
one week ago. A request the home help denied after their vicious
argument that morning.
No harm done, good feelings all around.
This feeling evaporated when she stopped me from entering her
home with her hand and a warning on each knuckle.
'Hold on a minute: we've a thief.'
She walked to the kitchen to produce the evidence ... a crust.
In the following seconds I was accused of eating all four loaves,
thus leaving her hungry, high and dry without tomorrow's
breakfast.
In her mind I committed this crime, under her nose,
despite my all day absence ... *weasel face.*

Once the squeals and slander ended; a bottle of milk vanished too.
Oddly I was cleared of this: the disappearance was, as she calmly
put it herself,
'Very strange.'
'Maybe you've hid it somewhere you can't remember?' I asked.
'NO!'
In support of my theory, I showed her the flood of milk seeping out
from under the fridge, and pointed down to the white cream,
moating the souls of our feet. With more squeals she denied
hiding
that bottle of milk which rolled around the bottom of the fridge,
half empty, half spilled ... far from my use.

At bedtime I discovered the kidnapped loaves, beheaded into her
carrier bag at the back of the wardrobe, where the cheese hid
once,
along with the birthday chocolates, all buried beneath a pile of
laundry ... far from my use. Nothing else vanished from that week;
the arguments remained as constant as ever. Using our old
reliable
method of accusation and denial, we thrashed out our hatred and
restrained every violent thought and swear word.
Last night the loaves were shifted from their hostage hideout to a
safer place under the commode in her room, beside that radiator.

They remained there in darkness until she released them first thing this morning, after one week of decay.
'Fresh!' She beamed, offering me a slice.
'Fresh from the ovens this morning!'

Can you believe that?

SHORT SCENE ONE

Lazily she yawns, smacks her lips and looks up to the clock calling it a liar: a morning nap dragged on into a long hapless sleep through afternoon.
Fearlessly, deftly she extracts her teeth, spits on them before rubbing them up and down her soup stained frock: the coconut from a morning scone lingers under her plastic palette
for hours and needs removing.
.....*Besides the water tap was so very far away.*
Minutes later, still alive here in the present day, she stands, walks into the kitchen and unwraps a fresh, pure block of butter
and handles it with her wet fingers into the dish.

After this she turns slowly, precise and tank-like on one track
and heads for the lavatory to perform whatever old women perform in there ... however messy.
And then with these same mauling hands ...
she hobbles towards ... to handle all the food I used to eat.

DOCTOR'S DAUGHTER - LABOURER'S SON

The key rattled ... the door opened ... she entered. Her eyes searched the room for focus, without co-ordination or luck. The cheap sherry (they told her was expensive) hit hard. "Yiz..." Grandmother had, that afternoon attended the wedding of her distant grandson who married into prosperity; *a Doctor's daughter no less!* Well, that end of the family were expected to shine, this union was the sparkling seal on his/her golden future. A doctor's daughter! Uncle told everyone. In his mind, the wedding was a complete validation of the noble blood which ran through his veins: and none of ours. Uncle had it, born with it ... nobility breeds nobility, she was only the first noble bride his children would secure. Others were to come.

Grandmother was honoured to be a guest at the momentous union, with these magnanimous people and wore an arrogant expression all day, a grimace created by the stiff bottom lip she used in the wedding photographs ... It was still about her face even after she transformed back into her pauper's clothes and smell.

"Oh ..." She rubbed her nose clean, exhaled the way old women do just before they speak with authority.
"Yes ... my son (the uncle) can put on quite a do ... yes..."

"Can he ... yeah ..." I replied, not looking from my book. The unfamiliar air of booze lingered about her, on her clothes and breath.
"Aye." She snapped, in keeping with her habit. At the wedding, in front of the in-laws *yes* was 'Yes .. Yes' or even 'Yiz.'

Life on a council estate is like this, the inhabitants are only too glad to revere a middle class position, give it respect and act differently in the presence of its' holder. Women such as grandmother often become a parody of the upper classes; fumbling with dainty biscuits and a thousand servile *thank yous*. The wrinkles around her face, usually deep and ingrained became stretched, taut, red and sore from smiling all day. What had uncle subjected her to? Did he not know that his mother could not physically smile? And did he not realise that her funny looking grimace with the curly edges was her smile?

When the royal in-laws arrived over to meet his mother, expecting her to be of the great character he claimed, uncle crouched down by her side and whispered through gritted teeth.

"Smile for the nice people mum ..."

Grandmother called from the kitchen ... through a trail of cheap perfume she left on the way in there. "Do you want coffee?" What ever happened to tea? From the kitchen she returned holding two dainty cups of instant coffee, (reserved for special occasions) placed on two mis-matching saucers which rattled with the left over nerves of having to perform all day. The old woman was tense and recoiling, uncle had twisted and twisted months before the wedding, rehearsing her into a presentable standard. I heard him.

"Don't show us up here ... mum ... these are nice people."

No matter how much he tried, her face was nothing but hard working class, Celtic stone. Not lace, nothing so refined. Beside the coffee, a Rich Tea biscuit soaked up the spills. I had hoped grandmother would have dropped the pretence by now, she did not need to perform for me. The after taste of that cheap/expensive Sherry prolonged the performance and played with her sense of priority and direction.

"Yiz ... dear ... it was marvellous ... quite a show ... marvellous. They had everything ... cakes! Fancy buns! Marvellous!" Her accent was proud and loud.

"Yeah."   "Yeeesss"

Uncle, a labourer by profession, had one misgiving and that was that he acted as if *he* managed, built up the firm which he worked for. Not only that, he tried to convince the rest of his relatives the same thing. Often there was confusion among his brothers as to what position he really held with that firm he spoke of with such importance. His *mum* was the only person who forgot the true nature of his class and position: like him, she expected all others to do the same.

It was an insult to her, personally, ifanyone remembered, or mentioned his occupation: an insult she rebuked with a claim that her son was a good honest worker, no matter what job he did.

"Yes ... my son certainly knows how to put on quite a do ..."

"Yeah." I replied

"Yeeesss ... it was full of nice people ... well mannered people who knew how to be polite and pleasant."

The ingredients of her visit across the door were reiterated with harsh pride, a true monarch pride which belied, denied her anti-monarch upbringing. Out of boredom I rested my head upon a pillow and stretched along the settee, the throne of soggy smells sat across from me and still those odours came, ebbing and flowing out from under her cushions in an invisible wave of awkward pungency. She continued ... of course. The voice louder, more proud than ever.

"There was nice little girls there ... dancing ... full of life ... going around everybody and talkin' ... (pause) the bride was beautiful ... a vision all in white."

"Yeah." I tried not to hear and focused half of my mind on the book in hand, the other half was at the wedding.

"Her father's a doctor ... I hear." "Is he yeah ...?"

"Yiz, maybe the doctor has a daughter for you .. or even a son for your sister ... and then maybe we can all get a piece of it!"

"No thanks." "NAH!!" She impersonated my voice, my disinterest. The grimace returned, without the false curly edges, her temper was well and truly blown.

"Nah ... that family ... (the doctor's) ... that decent family wouldn't have anything to do with yours ... BECAUSE YOUR FILTHY FAMILY -"
I intervened on the venom, not giving her the opportunity to requite the snobbery. "BULLSHIT!!"

After a very brief interval of unexpected calm and silence, my book flew across the room with light speed. The noble wedding guest held my face down on the pillow with her Celtic, hard man's fist. Our eyes locked in mutual, honest hatred. She pushed harder, down on my cheek bone, down on my resistance with all the force of her ninety five years, in an attempt to drive out the demons she saw. That face, the grimace had mutated beyond all earthly description into a salty bag of oatmeal and sausages.

Bestial unbeauty. And now the warning.
"IF YOU TALK TO ME LIKE THAT AGAIN ... I'LL BUSTYER FACE!!"
That squeal added another high note to the top of the scale. Before she emancipated my cheek from her bony brand, she pushed a little harder down for the bruising with all her sadistic might.

On my way out the door, escaping, I imagined grandmother at the wedding, so grand, her bald head chatting awkwardly to the doctor's daughter, the cause of all this.

"Oh certainly ... oh yeeesss ... hum ho ha hummm ho ho ha ... oh I always do that dear. Do you! Ha ha ha! Oh yeeesss."

And I imagined the doctor's daughter speaking to her groom, the labourer's son.

"Oh husband ... you never told me your grandmum was such a wonderful woman. Darling sweetest ... is she really ninety-five? And so pleasant too."

All impressions formed and given between the two families are wrong:
this marriage will not last.

SHORT SCENE TWO

I came down from my room to visit the bathroom
just as Uncle Daniel was sorting out the groceries with
grandmother ... in silence of course.
His wife Margaret sat in the next room watching the television
... also in silence.
I passed her on my way back from the bathroom.
Her grey hair had thinned even more since I last saw her
sitting there a week ago, rattling the same car keys ... waiting for
her husband to finish.
Years ago, when her children were around, she was quite adept at
interpreting to the old woman her husband's short temper
into polite questions and reasoning: but now seeing
as Daniel and his mother had fallen into a numb calm
with age; they no longer argued. Margaret jangled the keys.

"It's a lovely day ... isn't it .."

"Yeah Margaret ... lovely ..."

I closed the door and returned to my room. *The stranger.*
In the days of their arguments Margaret put into practice the
rationale she acquired as a sociology student years ago, years
before she married uncle and his mother,
But now in the light of this numb calm her services are
redundant.Yet still, every Friday she sits there rattling the car keys
... talking weather and waiting for her husband.

Get out Margaret.

UNCLE, NEPHEW, MOTHER AND SON

The uncle and the grandmother loomed from the nephew's immediate horizon, bent over and screaming at each other. It was a most difficult sight to behold; a three foot woman and her five foot middle aged son locked in the bitterest of confrontations on the bleary horizon of a council estate at three o'clock on a Sunday afternoon. His cry echoed off the slate roofs like a yodel from the Alps.

"Ya fuckin' oul headcase!"

The doors leading up to the circus sight could not pass quick enough for the young nephew approaching with growing concern, for he knew of his uncle's infamous temper and of his grandmother's infamous manner. Given this genetic mixture, it would only be a matterof time before mother and son came to blows. Indeed it would be a matter of time before the neighbourhood would witness the sight of the old woman's fat frame falling under the boot of her insane old son. The nephew quickened his pace into a slow run. At the third door down the uncle's entreat became clear.

"Har did ya do it!!"

Not four hours ago mother and son were having Sunday lunch in the garden of his home, he thought it would be a nice treat for her to sit outside in the sun. For that time, both seemed at ease with each other despite their anaemic complexions. The uncle bent lower, his complexion red and visible to the help at hand.

"Do what uncle?" The nephew asked.
"We're locked out!!" "Eh?"

"WE'RE LOCKED OUT can you not hear? You're as deaf as she is!"
To make matters worse the pensioner repeated this to the nephew.

"We're locked out!!" Everyone in the estate who had heard the family and their troubles came out to watch with both bold eyes. The grandmother called out to the air in the hope of God looking down. "We're locked out!!" No one moved to help or even inquire. The mother, son and nephew looked around with an embarrassed panic.

"Pat! Pat ... we're locked out." Her old neighbour next door raised his arms and let them fall again for fear of rescue spoiling his only excitement in years. The uncle turned from forcing the door with all his might: face red, full of pumping rage he spoke to his nephew with embarrassed shame and anger.

"In the name of Christ, d'ya hear her...!" Oblivious to the embarrassment she caused, the grandmother continued to call to the air, to the neighbourhood, to their enemies.

"WE'RE LOCKED OUT ... YO HO ... BITTY WE'RE LOCKED OUT."

"ALRIGHT FOR CHRIST'S SAKES MUM!!!"

In keeping with the spirit which saw her through both world wars, she folded her arms beneath her breasts, watched the chaos with a stiff smile and laughed in spite of this insult, in the face of exposure. "Ho ho - I'm gonna have to sleep out in a field the night ... ha ... ha"

If truth be told she enjoyed the idea of sleeping rough, it would break the boredom of the years and provide a ripe opportunity to prove that she was not done. Those who passed by, those who (by rule) avoided the family, she stopped and delivered a briefing of the siege with the invisible ghost who jammed the door and refused to submit. The old woman then walked off in search of assistance ... really this was a thin excuse to escape from her son, after all she had endured (like very few) the brunt of his insane temper whenever their 'coffee mornings' went horribly wrong.

The uncle stepped back, insulted the door and charged it with all force. His nephew stood in abject abeyance, not knowing whether to move away from the charging uncle or to give help. The banging and shuddering awoke the remaining few who dozed through the commotion. BANG! BANG! Flushed and exhausted with the last kick, his glasses fell to the floor, the uncle struggled but they fell. His nephew laughed. A voice returned from the other end of the street. It was a voice laced with warbling nerves and an awful stupidity years old. It was as they dreaded, the voice of the old woman. Even she had heard the bangs.

"DON'T BREAK MY DOOR ... DON'T BREAK MY DOOR!!"

He had had enough.   "Look mum, I'm goin' home ..."

"But what about -"   "I've got a golf mat -"   "EH?"

" I SAID I'VE GOT A GOLF MATCH ... MUM ... GOLF MATCH!!!"

No person in that area played such a game, those who did were advised by an unwritten law, by an inherent law to keep the activity quiet. To the neighbourhood this activity was a hall mark of the middle classes, therefore an overt declaration of superiority. When he screamed, he knew the secret life was out, exposed by the anger in his genes.

"I'm gettin' outta here (for this he forced a tougher accent) she'd drive me fuckin' nuts. Year after year ... Sunday after Sunday."
It was no use, as with all famous partners in history, the mother and son were joined by a tense chord.

"WHERE YA GOIN'? WHAT ABOUT ME!!"

The uncle close to tears screamed. "WHAT THE HELL CAN I DO ABOUT IT!!!"

The neighbourhood watched intently, a few came out with mugs of tea so as to relax with the show totally.

"Well you can't leave me here!"

"BUT THERE'S NOTHIN' I C -"

"EH?" The hearing aid buzzed and squealed in her ear, interrupting vital communication between. The uncle strained in making his desire perfectly clear. But how could he discreetly convey the urgency of a golf match to his deaf old mother in the middle of a council estate which hated his guts.

Temper permitting, he tried using the language of fingers on palms and short swings through the air with his imaginary club.

"LOOK MUM. LISTEN!! I'VE GOT A GOLF MATCH TO PLAY IN TEN MINUTES. UNDERSTAND! I CAN'T HANG AROUND HERE ALL DAY, I'VE GOT A GOLF MATCH!!"

His mother looked up, cupped the hearing device (although her hearing was perfect) and provided the answer.

"Maybe you could get a piece of cardboard ... and -"
"CARDBOARD!" The old woman jumped with fright, her hearing suddenly restored. "ARE YOU FUCKIN' STUPID ... CARDBOARD TO OPEN THAT BIG WOODEN DOOR ... (he turned to the nephew) HAVE YOU EVER HEARD SUCH BULLSHIT."

This strong language shocked the nephew, he had heard them argue before, but never before had either resorted to swearing. It was surprising that the mother let this *'filth'* go unchecked.

"Right you ... come here ..."   "Where?"
The nephew followed his uncle to the back of the house.

Watching the boy ascend up the ladder to the little roof outside his old room, the uncle spoke with authority upon the objects of the detour; it was a dream realised to be giving orders. For sometime now he had been a labourer with the same firm. The card he punched in with lay in his overall thirty years this April. Everyday as the stamps accumulated, it reminded and embarrassed him of his middle class pretence. To dinner guests the uncle made a joke of his occupation or described it eloquently as *'extensive construction assistant.'* However when too much Claret washed away a pleasantly prepared meal, he lied totally.

The ladder shook under the convulsive weight of the young lad, with every space climbed and conquered, the foreman's face decreased in size but his voice boomed louder than ever.

"FOR CHRIST'S SAKES HURRY UP ... IT'S ONLY A SMALL ROOF ... BE A MAN!"

The plan was elementary; with the stone provided the nephew was to break the window, climb down and unjam the jammed door. To hurry and banish all natural reservation his nephew may have had, the order came from below.

"Put it through ... that's right ... harder!" The lad obliged. THUD. THUD. "That's it son ... a little bit harder and we're home ..."

The nephew looked down to his uncle's thick glasses reflecting the Sunday light. Dry scrapes of hair pulled from either side of the foreman's head ... an effect that crowned the ugliness below.

"JUST PUT THE FUCKIN' BRICK THROUGH THE WINDOW!!"

"That's enough (the mother warned her outsized son) .. watch your language. Don't use that talk near me. Keep it for your wife."

"EH! You'd drag bad talk out of a fuckin' saint!" In the privacy of the backyard, he felt safe abusing her. This venue was at least a little more private than the front gate. The misunderstanding began again.

"I never dragged you out here! You come down here every Sunday the way you always do! Whether I want you to come down or not!" "Mum ... look ... (it was the calm approach now) ... I didn't say tha-" "No dear ... I dragged you nowhere. If it were my choice I wouldn't come near you at all!" Her independence became a personal crusade pursued with a hard face. All help offered was taken as an affront. This was the secret of her everlasting life.

"Mum ... please ... listen ... I didn't say that -" The grandmother turned to the nephew, aware of the misunderstanding.

"Did ya hear him! ... I dragged him down here! Anybody would think I'd die without you and yer wee Sunday afternoons!" She repeated this in an exaggerated accent, a tactic designed to belittle the other's position or hospitality. "YOU AND YER WEE SUNDAY AFTERNOONS!!" She waved her arms in the air, another battle tactic of hers for God knows what. "YOU AND YER WEE SUNDAY AFTERNOONS!!"

Her son had had enough of the misunderstanding.

"WILL YOU LISTEN TO ME MUM!!"

"AYE! Go on ..."

"Mum nobody dragged anybody anywhere. Okay!"

"Aye!"

"Okay!"

"I suppose you tell your wife ... HER ... that I drag -"

"NO MUM! YOU ALWAYS GET THE WRONG END OF THE STICK!"

"EH? WHAT THE HELL ARE YOU SAYIN'?" She fiddled again with the perfectly functional hearing aid. Again to clarify the impossible to the intolerable, the uncle broke the sentence down. The words fell down, out of his mouth in dense aggressive slabs of a Belfast accent.

"I SAID YOU - ALWAYS - GET - THE - WRONG - END - OF - THE - STICK! Mum ..."

"EH?" "MUM THE STICK!"

"WHAT STICK?" A new comer to this situation could easily be fooled by her show of deafness, and the pretend humour she thought it created. But not her son.

"Nathin' mum ... ya mad fuckin' oul bastard ..."

The invisible cord which bound them, also restrained them from violence. The glasses sparkled the command once more.

"Put the brick through the window. Right through!"

THUD! THUD! THUD! The biscuit crumbled, the window fell in shatters on to the floor of the vacant room.

The remaining hard cement core fell on to the slates of the little roof, exploding into an avalanche of dangerous rocks. The soft bulb of the grandmother took shelter immediately, the way she did in the 'Blitz'. Her son, the uncle, consumed with rage, was less fortunate. A rock, the last one, the biggest of all bounced down the slates and aimed itself with precision. The missile followed the air path with a sense of purpose as if willing to take its' part in history, it made contact with the uncle and his glasses. THUD.

     His mother ran behind the disaster, trying to steal a look at the gore. He ran out into his car and sped off ... never to return for two weeks.
That was his misfortune, that was his life, that was his job and that was him.
He had to endure time with all its' unrequited injustices (like his being a labourer instead of a foreman) until death ... and then pretty soon ... that would be all.

IN THE AFTERNOON

In the afternoon it began raining,
Soaking the estate with a wet gloom
That was just unnecessary and unfair
To the already-damp lives there.

I walked home to Grandmother's,
Her television was turned up very loud:
I took the remote control from her hand
And switched the sound off.

She made no objections as I flicked
Through the stations.
Afternoon viewing mostly,
Loud bright fantasies for the unemployed.

Finally we settled on snooker
And she sat watching with me,
Rolling her thumbs and whispering a Rosary
Until the silence of the afternoon

And the heat of the fire drugged her.
Once again she bowed her head into her frock
And slept a dummy run for death:
Most of our afternoons passed this way.

A CHICKEN FOR A CHRISTMAS DINNER

It was five o'clock and dark outside with festive poise. Liam and his brother had spent the day working on a roof in Magherafelt: sleet and lashing rain curbed any progress they made on the tiling of that roof.

Liam stood, sighed and nodded a grimace of frustration for his lack of pay. The little wages he'd earned, he gambled on a horse, which was (unknown to him) running its last race on its last legs.

Tezzie cursed her son's stupidity, but gave him five pound from her pension: three weeks money, one extra week, a Christmas bonus she neither expected nor wanted back. The warmth of the grate wafted a haze from Liam;s damp and soiled working jeans. And folding the note with shame, he promised his mother that the money would go to good use: a chicken for a Christmas dinner. Opening the door to leave, Liam told us that a turkey was just too expensive and large for himself. He closed the gate on the way back home.

"He misses her." Tezzie spoke.

"He misses who?" I begged.

"His wife! His wife!"

She yelled only to conceal the watery emotion filling her eyes. It was then I remembered that this was Liam's first Christmas alone, without a wife, for she had left home two week before; fleeing to England on a new lease of life. Wiping her eyes, Tezzie consoled herself with hope:

"I think she's softening though ... cause she sent him a new pair of socks."

One pair of socks in exchange for forty years of marriage?

Liam's gambles never paid off.

A WORD OR TWO ON THE SUCCESS OF MR. JEAN CLAUDE VAN DAMME

A rare television premier of a Jean Claude Van Damme film was to be screened that night on Ulster Television: my brothers went quietly over the moon about this and encouraged me to suspend my disbelief in Mr. Van Damme's script and enjoy the film, bearing in mind that there was nothing much else to do, and that anything was better than another night of fighting grandmother. Put like this, I too got a little excited and went *quietly over the moon* ... In this way Television and Hollywood have us: Their films are, by and large, rubbish. Yet, you find yourself watching them with a certain degree of concentration and belief, simply because there is nothing else to concentrate upon ... except each other.

At grandmother's, you either watch a film or argue all night with her, or among each other. There is nothing sadder than the silence of three grown men who have just saw too much of each other and have had enough. We arrived early, all prepared and eager for the excitement. When I told her about the action, muscles and plot, she bounced up and ran over to Winnie, who also shared her passion for action adventures. Being half blind, Winnie loved how the blurs on the screen moved faster. *At least that was something.* We counted the hours down to the start of the film; making tea and chatting amicably ourselves ... not one argument in sight. Even grandmother joined in on the cheer, airing for the tenth time those anecdotes from the O.A.P. club. And as we sat watching the film, our minds lifted from the wet streets of West Belfast and travelled to the golden sunshine of America, far far away. And we joined in with full emotion as Van Damme kissed many women, fought many men and caught the real villain in the end.

The lights went up, we yawned and stretched; sighing and commenting on the film, throwing fake punches all around. Grandmother rubbed her eyes and exclaimed amazement at the late hour. I turned the television off as she walked off to bed, leaving us with a final comment on the film:

"Well it killed a few hours for us at least. It put the night in."
She was right: Thank you Mr. Van Damme. Thank you.

BEFORE BED

"Ah I've had enough ..."
She said as she stood, undressing slowly, disarming
 herself
before bed. Removing the glasses first, she swore
that she couldn't take much more of this place:

Day in and out and all the time.
So she laid her glasses in the same place as always,
In an organised pile along with her hearing aid and false
 teeth.
It demeans her depending on inventions for sight, hearing
 and taste.

Towards the door she bid us all a toothless goodnight
And apologised for being unable and not much company.
Sometimes I help her heavy-footed march climb each
stair whenever the light on the landing has gone out;

Check her breathing before bed, fetch another glass of
water to place beside the statue under the votive lamp.
And often I help her feet back in when they stray out
from under the quilt into the cold.

Tomorrow she'll wake up groggy and disorientated ...
Feeling that the day now begins without her: which it does.

BANG AND CLATTER #1

At three in the morning the radio ended, I switched it off,
Rearranged the blankets and turned over to face the wall.
Failing this, I then turned left to face the contents of the
        room:
but either way proved useless.

And then the groans came, accompanied by
The bang and clatter of her commode next door ...
Through the walls of our neighbouring rooms,
Paper-thin at that hour of the morning.

Grandmother has made a habit of these meanderings
Through night, whenever sleep or the Novenna to
Blessed Jude fails her. These nightly games of Blind
man's Bluff help keep her groggy, nasty and bitterly

Jealous of my normal ten hours sleep.
Her view is this; if she can't get to sleep
In her own house, in her own bed, then she
Sure as hell won't let anyone else.

So she banged and clattered louder,
With the commode and its brown plastic rim,
Reliving for real this time the drill of the district nurse.

Determined to last out her spite, I lay on: there was no
need to rush in and check her welfare ...
It could wait till morning.

BANG AND CLATTER #2

The bang and clatter came again, this time caught off
Guard, I rose from my sleep to see who her attacker was.

You've got to check every little noise when they're that age.
Through a crack in the door I saw her mumbling.

Rubbing her bald head and cursing the wet confusion.
Then she turned, full face in the glare of a night light

And searched through the drawers, passed the medications
And rubs for *any oul rag,* having found one,

She turned around and dug her hand down deeper,
Drying in the darkness where she was split in half.

I came away regretting the sight ...
Not for the first time.

FOREVER MODERNE MARGARET

It was a Sunday evening around half seven and, for late September, still bright. After dinner Margaret and her husband Daniel relaxed in their lounge; she with her Catherine Cookson, he with his Sunday Times. The tail end of 'Songs of Praise' flickered devotion on the bubble screen of their old fashioned television set. Daniel had turned the sound down to a faint but glorious mumble. Having watched that particular episode before, a repeat of the Easter Special, Margaret did not mind the sound being low. What she did mind though was having such an outdated, cumbersome article. It embarrassed her: all her friends at the keep fit evening class had brand new television sets, the latest model of the latest modern appliances.

Not only that, Margaret felt that it looked so out of place among the fairly new decor which they, or rather she, strove hard to keep modern. She had seen the latest model while browsing in town for the perfect gift to give her daughter Sarah, who had just moved in with her boyfriend Tim. This was another thing that gave her heartburn, the fact that her daughter and *this man* were living in sin; despite her wishes, despite her warnings. It soon smoothed out though when - over coffee - Sarah and Tim persuaded her that her attitude to their great union was like her television set: old fashioned, outdated and in the way. So in keeping with the times, forever modern, Margaret and Daniel revised their moral beliefs and subsequently all their difficulties with Protestant Tim, to the extent that an open invitation to visit was theirs for the taking ... *any time; just call in.*

Well, besides all Margaret's friends at the over fifties keep fit class were Protestants, and all Dan's friends at the county Golf club were Protestants too. In fact, now that Margaret thought about it, half of their friends had daughters or sons who were living in sin. This issue became a cosy common ground over the sectarian divide in their outgoings.

Margaret found it a pleasure to visit Sarah's and Tim's love nest: it was like visiting the home of a new friend. While Margaret marvelled at the crazy decor her daughter had chosen, Daniel discussed - over Cognac - Wives & Sport with his illegitimate son-in-law. Another visit had been arranged for this coming Monday ...

"Dan...?" Margaret asked.
"Yes love ...?" He replied, looking at her over the bent corner of his Sunday Times for a clearer view.

"Does mum (his mother) know about Sarah and Tim?"

"What that he's a Prod?" Annoyed, Margaret tutted.

"He's not a Prod Dan! The term is Protestant!"

"Okay Margaret ... what d'ya want t'know?" Replied Daniel, his face a little flushed by the stern nature of her correction.

"Does mum know about Sarah and Tim living together?"

"Well ... no ... but she knows that he's a Protestant: nothing else. Why?"

"Well Dan, you know how your mother behaves ... she may well embarrass us if she thinks that there's something going on between them. I just think that it's better if we just left her behind tomorrow evening." Daniel put the paper down, fold it with slow care, with the full knowledge that such a suggestion warranted careful, elaborate discussion: he did not want to force his mother upon anyone, let alone upon his new found friend Tim.

"But Margaret, I've already invited her ... sure she's all set."

"Hmmmm." Margaret replied, satisfied; her husband's tone of voice was one of passive agreement, not one of aggression. She took off her pince-nez and played with the royal blue silk cord. Two grey footprints remained on the sides of her nose, deep and ingrained, even though she had only worn them for a matter of minutes. Her skin was too old these days to withstand the slightest wear and tear. Margaret sipped her coffee - modern Cappuccino - and cradled it in both hands. The evening sun made everything in the lounge glow with season.

"Daniel, ... would you mind if we left her behind tomorrow evening?"

Her accent bore the unmistakable air, that tuneful lilt of being forced: the working class sound of her vowels, naturally there, were submerged in favour of the high, polite brightness of the middle class pronunciation.

"I don't mind what you do ... But what are we gonna tell her though?"

His accent had remained crude: it was just the use of certain words in his vocabulary, and his ideals, which had changed.

"I'll call down tomorrow after work and tell her that its off," replied Margaret.

"Och, sure the old woman is much too proud to ask me why." She replaced her pince-nez and placed the cup on a coaster on the reproduction table; the sight of which reminded her again that the time had come to redecorate.

"What time did Tim say to meet him at the restaurant?"

"About half eight."

They both returned to their reading.

THEIR ARDGLASS
(for Abbon - son of the fair haired woman)

I took from her fingers the broken earring and pushed it carefully through a wrinkle in her lobe. She had struggled with it in front of the mirror since seven o'clock that morning: the going-away nerves ruined the co-ordination normally required. It was a 'Red Letter Day' for her, even the bottle of perfume from Bundoran was given its first taste of air, in liberal splashes around her clothes, around the house like holy water. Unwrapping a rolled up tissue, she produced the other earring, which was just as cheap and awkward to fit as its partner had been. They were a *lousy oul gift* that had gone unnoticed. "Where y'goin'?" "Ah nowhere son ... only on an oul trip to Ardglass ... that's all. Nathin' special y'know."

It was traditional for the Nuns to give the pensioners of that parish their first taste of summer air. Word of the excursion to the coast and the many stops on the way was released months before hand, so as to allow the older, slower women of the parish the chance to enrol early for the home perm service which the *blessed* Nuns also ran.

That morning, dressed in a royal red cardigan and a brown polyester frock, she walked around the house, unable to sleep any longer; counting the hours since dawn and full of the emotions she took pride in hiding; happiness ... love. "It's only an oul thing run by the Nuns ... nathin' really. Nathin' t'get excited about." Whether it was an excursion to America or a day trip to Ardglass, the distance was irrelevant to those infirm at home.

"Winnie's goin' with me. It was her idea more than mine. She likes these things, wee breaks ... days out." No trip out of the house seemed fit or fair without the company of her old only friend Winnie. Like lovers they had sworn to each other months before-hand to share the backseat of the bus, coming and going: *swear t'God!* Their request was put forward to the Nuns in time and was granted immediately because of Winnie's bad leg or good acting. They were so pleased. Grandmother liked to tell tales of this alliance in tones which fobbed it off as something silly ... childish, as if they had both surpassed the age of companionship ... as if they should have known better. Because of the shame, she tried to hide the warmth the relationship generated in her.

"I don't feel like goin', but Winnie begged me. Y'know har she gets ... can't have a shite without me there to wipe her arse." I walked into the bathroom, happy for her, pleased for Winnie: happy that they had both found something to replace their missing husbands. She sat down in the armchair, waiting patiently, reeking of scent, with four long hours to kill. A thin hair net had been added to the preparation, carefully webbing in place her brittle white fuzz. It was impossible for her to make any sudden movement, for fear of the brand new perm falling out around her shoulders in clumps. She looked at the clock, turning her head as if she had no neck and tutted, certain that Winnie was lying in bed across the street; her curtains still drawn to the estate. *What a sleeper!* She tutted again for this lie-in illustrated Winnie's true lack of enthusiasm for their only decent outing in years; this lack of enthusiasm evinced the fact that Winnie's life was therefore a great deal fuller, more whole. As a favour I offered to knock on Winnie's door, hard, to get her up early for the excitement. Grandmother was so pleased. It was love between the two old friends, no matter how much she tried to disguise the feeling.

"Are you comin' back here t'day?" She asked. "Yeah."

"Well then you can let yerself in ... you'll probably be in before me." I walked back and took the key from her hand. Her disguised feelings of warmth, enthusiasm surfaced again as we exchanged jokes. "When I get in you can make me a cup of tea. Ha ha!" I in turn told her not to be getting drunk and not to be bringing back any strange men and that I had heard about these pensioner trips ... *lots of booze and dancing.*

"What! At my time of day! Go on with ye! Are ya mad!" Looking at her happiness, exchanging those jokes grandmother and I almost liked each other. I kissed the hair net on her head, staining my lips with the sting of lacquer all day long: a reminder of just how special her day out was. After a routine of good-byes I finally left. She called out another important message. "EXPECT ME BACK LATE T'NITE ... THESE TRIPS DRAG ON." Her laugh and subsequent smile disappeared behind the lace curtains. We waved again, *just to make sure* and I walked off thinking that the Nuns who had organised this trip for the infirm were guaranteed their place in Heaven...

2

Two, three or four hours later I returned in time to see her bus depart from the street. They were all in there, the black and white of the Nuns; the excursionists, all crammed up to the window like balls of cotton wool. Winnie and grandmother were lost somewhere at the back of the coach, but I waved anyway at the sight of a familiar green mac ...

When I entered the empty house, I found her sitting where I had left her sitting hours before. She seemed as surprised as me.

"What are y'doin' here granny?" She turned her head away without answering, curling her lip up at its corner in disgust.

"Granny what happened?" She jerked her head away from my caress, not caring now whether or not the precious perm stayed in place. The earrings swung from her lobes, large and foolish. *What use was jewellery to her now?* She reached for them and struggled once again with the thin wire catches. Before any damage was done I took the earrings out for her, using the same care I had put them in with. Could it have been that she had forgotten about the trip? Wasn't there enough room on the bus? Had she abdicated her seat beside Winnie because of a last minute argument? No. The rest of the excursionists had abandoned her, stabbed her memory: those Nuns ... those Devils. The thought of Winnie enjoying an ice cream on the pier with some other neighbour frightened her: that trip might have been her last chance before death to enjoy a summer excursion with an old friend. There was winter to endure and that was very trying for a pensioner of ninety-six to endure. There was no optimism about her face, not now. The next trip to Ardglass was one year away. I knelt down beside her, not daring to touch a hand or hair of hers.

"Granny?" "What!" She finally replied.

"I thought you were goin' t'Ardglass t'day?"

"They never bloody well came for me! All right! Are ya satisfied nigh? Nosy!" This outburst proved that she was (regrettably) very much back to her old time self; back again to the same character which saw her abandoned.

"Granny ... did you -"

"ARE YA DEAF! I SAID THEY NEVER BLOODY WELL CAME FOR ME! FER GOD'S SAKES! THEY PROMISE YE ONE THING AND THEN DON'T BATHER THEIR ARSE GIVEN IT TILL YE!!" By rolling it all, words and venom into one foul breath, she had exhausted herself. Amazed, I pressed on, to gain knowledge, a reason for this.

"But why didn't they -" She interrupted me again, anticipating my *annoying, stupid question.* "HAR THE HELL DO I KNOW!!" After that she sat staring out at the empty estate, watching the ghosts of the pensioners take her seat on the bus like a cuckoo. There was a valid explanation as to why the Nuns had abandoned her in particular, but it was just too tiresome to convey to that faulty hearing aid and tetchy ear. Besides, how could she understand? How could I tell her that, after the last trip to Ardglass, which she supposedly spoiled for all the others, the Benevolent Sisters swore *never again.* They had all of the other pensioners to consider.

Pushing out the bottom layer of her teeth and sucking them back in again with slow poise, she mulled over the betrayal. Who was the Judas? "I bet ye it was her from next door, (she nodded her head towards the wall) sheez never firgivin me for that last trip." Realistically it could have been anyone, even Winnie.

"Aye I bet it was her. But I know what I'll do on her the next time I see her (she squinted her eyes like an old witch doctor casting a spell) I'll creep up on her and put her straight on a few things." She stood and took off the royal red cardigan, sighing more of that hidden sorrow. "I'll soon get her back son. Nah don't you worry about it. Sheez fir the high jump." After this she disappeared into the kitchen, into the neighbouring bathroom to retrieve from the floor her everyday clothes, discarded there at dawn, in a fit of early excitement. "Ah I'm not bathered about their oul trip t'Ardglass ..." A voice from the bathroom sang pride and spite, loud enough for the whole of Ardglass to hear.

"THEY CAN ALL STICK IT UP THEIR ARSE!"

THE KING BENEATH THE CLOCK

Beneath the glory of a brass clock
The rabbit marvelled with glazed eyes,

Just challenged: forever alert for a robbing hand.
Guarded by two figurines the gaudy king sat,

Squat on a reign of tiles, silently still on its delft
behind
from which it shit coins on my needy days.

OUR GRANDMOTHER'S 95th

Sarah my cousin, uncle's daughter, and lover to Tim
Came down one night on a rare visit: our grandmother's
    95th.
Armed with a legend of gifts, trailing Tim behind her,
Sarah opened the door with a coo-ee and an exclamation

On how much I had grown since the last time.
That's who Sarah saw herself as; full of fun, the life
And soul of the cousins. She didn't visit us that often,
When she did she tried desperately to disprove her
    reputation

Among us as the stranger and the snob, by imitating
The humour she mistook for ours. "How y'doin' there
Granny? A big 95 today!" Grandmother, in turn,
Imitated the humour she thought most fitting,

The humour she used over their odd Christmas dinners
    together.
"Oh I'm doin' fine. Still able to dance Sarah!"
To authenticate the joke, grandmother moved her arms
    about
Her side; looking surprised and happy, casually honoured.

She thanked Sarah for the silver wrapped gifts, but swore
That it was too much. In reply Sarah claimed that,
If she had have arrived empty handed, there would have
    been
A bloody big fight!

They all laughed at this, even Tim, even though he was
From the other side and couldn't possibly understand
The religion he was mixing with.
Our grandmother looked over at Tim and smiled:

He smiled back at her, she accepted him now,
ever since the day he took her on a drive through the
 country.
Tim smiled again, grandmother liked him now,
Despite his Protestant faith and *in-sin ways.*

While they spoke among themselves Sarah and I exchanged
Career talk. "What are you doin' with yourself now then?"
"Oh nathin' much Sarah ... just hangin' around." She
 walked
Into the kitchen and produced the cake: nine candles, nine

decades. "Where's your brother?" She asked, for they
Had had a terse exchange of sarcasm a while back,
On her last visit that summer. "He's at college in England
Sarah." I replied. "Oh is he! That's lovely."

"Tell me this ... is he the one granny doesn't like?"
"No Sarah," I replied, "That's me."
She laughed and excused her big mouth.
At that moment I looked over at grandmother:

That old woman talking ever-so-proper to Tim;
Fraternising now with all the things she once despised.
She smiled back and I left the party.

THE WAR CRIMES OF WINNIE

Over fifty years ago a woman called Winnie
Dragged out on to the street an old woman called Susan

And beat her black and blue for the entertainment of the
Neighbourhood. The old woman clawed and squealed

For help or mercy as Winnie continued to punch, kick and
bite. That was over *fifty* years ago, when Winnie was

A lot younger and Susan was my great grandmother.
To look at Winnie these days, old and infirm herself,

It's hard to believe such a crime of one so frail.
She often visits us now, ignoring the past the way old

War criminals do: all serene with old age, as if there's
nothing left of the cruelty that once drove her.

Whenever she visits I make a point of pushing past her,
Not handing over the respect she expects, holding a grudge

Tight, in the manner of my father, who was only a boy when
It happened. But us Quinns never forget ... even if
grandmother has.

MASS PALS

Every Thursday evening near seven, after Wednesday's
Absolution, the Mass Pals link and hump their aches

Towards the warm glow of a service. Using each other
As a crutch against the night, all weathers,

Their boredom and loneliness, their hobble back home
Is slow but bonding.

A NOTION OF THE FUTURE WITHOUT HER

I have an idea, a dread: my notion is
That when the old woman dies
Of whatever gets her first,
I will be the one nominated to clear out

And cleanse the house she leaves behind;
The house I live in now;
The house which nests everything,
Pads, wading and clothes:

All what was once important to her.
I have a guilty feeling that whenever I lay
Hands on her rubbish,
All her old skins for the bin,

I will suddenly regret every insult
I threw at her ... provoked or uncalled for.
I have an idea now,
That maybe I should go down to the living room,

Throw my arms around her before it's too late
And beg forgiveness for our faulty relationship.
But I know for sure that this would only
Scare or embarrass her.

I'll have to wait until I die
Before our reunion takes place in Heaven or Hell;
Depending on who the Lord decides
Was right or unjust.

THE SHIRT I GAVE HER

The shirt I gave her I bought for £10
In a second-hand shop in town.
The shirt I gave her had a light blue silk effect
And could have (very possibly) once belonged
To Al Capone or some Miami Warlord.
The shirt I gave her, I discarded over the chair
In her kitchen, where it lay for weeks without
Moving a sleeve.
Later when I picked it up to examine its potential
as luggage, the shirt I gave her stank of sweat,
Of her perfume.
The day before I left she asked me what I intended
To do with *such a lovely garment*.
I took it off the back of the chair and threw it into her.
She caught and smiled, stretched it out by the shoulders
And marvelled (this time in public) at the exquisite cut
And light blue silk effect.

The next morning I left,
The chair in her kitchen looked bare and abandoned;
But that shirt should look good upon
The hump of that 96 year old woman.

THREE MONTHS FREE

"Why can't y'stay here?" She asked.
"I can't granny ..."
Then she gave me a look, the kind that pleads
Don't leave when you know you have to,
Because you have been together for so long.
If she had've broken down and wept,
I believe I would still be there now,
In the middle of an afternoon, looking at her
On that armchair with her forever sore leg.

"Sure there's nathin' for ye in England.
They don't want ye!"
Then she gave me another look,
One confident of my failure and subsequent return to her
    door.
Her doubt of my success was just: I have returned
To her so many times after vowing that I would never be
    back.
But this time, my absence proves,
I've stayed away longer than she ever expected.

WHAT KEEPS HER

Now that I've deserted her
And gone to live in the land of my enemy,
Leaving her alone to ponder the silence
Of her nights and afternoons:

I suppose she will amble around my absence,
Awkward with yearning, until an accident befalls her
One night when the moon is low
And black frost has taken its spite out on her step.

Despite my relative guilt,
She will rise in the morning as ever,
Beat her egg in a cup with butter and wait
For the homehelp to come and light the fire.

If it has not been built
To her peculiar satisfaction,
She will use the temper she reserved for me ...
And survive.

CAUGHT SHORT

Caught short,
Urging a path through the early hours,
I switch on the light.
Her portrait above
The lamp below reminds me.
Poverty-edged,
Weather-aged,
She implores me
To post home the love absent
From our early morning goodbye.